Enchantée

ANGIE ESTES

Enchantée

Oberlin College Press
Oberlin, Ohio

The FIELD Poetry Series, vol. 31
Oberlin College Press, 50 N. Professor Street, Oberlin, OH 44074
www.oberlin.edu/ocpress

Cover and book design: Steve Farkas
Cover photograph: David Heald, "Entrance to the South Aisle, le Thoronet"
(gelatin silver print, 1986). Reproduced by permission of the artist.

Library of Congress Cataloging-in-Publication Data

Estes, Angie.
  [Poetry. Selections]
  Enchantée / Angie Estes.
      pages cm. — (The FIELD Poetry Series ; vol. 31)
   ISBN 978-0-932440-41-9 (pbk. : alk. paper) — ISBN 0-932440-41-X
(pbk. : alk. paper)
   I. Title.
   PS3555.S76A6 2013
   811'.54—dc23
                              2013032003

for Tamara

quella che 'mparadisa la mia mente

Contents

********** *Strutture della fase attuale visibili*
Structures that are visible

———————— *Strutture della fase attuale non visibili ma di posizione certa*
Structures not visible but about whose position we are
certain

++++++++ *Strutture della fase attuale ipotizzate*
Structures thought to have existed

Legend on excavation map below the
church of Santa Cecilia in Rome

While they sat together, there was an extraordinary mute passage be-
tween her vision of this vision of his, his vision of her vision, and her
vision of his vision of her vision.

Henry James, *What Maisie Knew*

⚜

Per Your Request,

gilded bronze rosettes once pressed
through the Pantheon's dome like stars

filling the coffers of the sky,
and history posed especially

for you, its spree become
repose. From the Janiculum hill

across the Tiber, you watched
the aureole settle around

its nipple as if a flying saucer
nestled among the rising

stones and called it
home. Wisteria still hopes

over every wall, holding it
in place, while the lantern of Sant'Ivo

screws into the sky. When the snakes
sacred to Asclepius arrived

on Isola Tiberina, they made themselves
at home on the floors of the temple

dedicated to healing: dogs were trained
to lick and snakes to flicker

their tongues over any ailing
part of the body. You always loved

the way a crow's
caw caw caw hangs

in the sky like a claw,
a crowbar that pries open

the day: a posse of roses coming
to possess you.

I Want to Talk About You

when starlings swell over Otmoor, east of Oxford, as the afternoon
light starts to fade. Fifty flocks of fifteen to twenty starlings, riff raff

who have spent the day foraging in fields and gardens suddenly rise
like a blanket tossed into the sky, a reveling that molts sorrows to roost

rows, roost rows to sorrows as they soar through aerial corridors and swerve
into the shape of a cowl that lengthens to a woolen scarf wrapping

and wrapping, nothing at the center but throat: thousands of single black notes
surge into a memory called *melody,* the lovers damned but driven on

by violent winds in *the cold season when starlings' wings bear them
along in broad and crowded ranks,* extended cadenzas to pieces that

never get played, brochure for the flared tip that begins with the tongue
and lips of the embouchure wrapping the saxophone's slurred

howl, scrawled signature of the sky. Thousands fly but never collide
in their pre-roost ritual, Dante's long list of God's works excited

raked left and right over leafless branches of trees until they
drop like the bodies of suicides, draped on thorns of the wild

thickets their cast-off souls become, unable to rise the way a wave
nearing shore will crest, something on the tip of its tongue

thrown back before it breaks and splays, starlings laid down
like the wave's rain of sand or words falling

out of a sentence: *art slings*, we called them, *grass lint, snarl gist, gnarls sit*. Art slings them this way, *last grins*, art slings swell, rove

over, red rover, red rover, send *artlings* right over, *artlings rove, moor to swell*, write Otmoor all over

Cache

Here lies a hectic site, la Cité
tête-à-tête with the Seine
while Notre Dame goes on rising
like the heel of God's boot.
Ancient Roman isle, river

flung around it like a lavender
orchid lei around a neck: here lies
the new moon with the old moon

in her arms. Voici the sheer
leers of else, ready for hire.
We filled the room
with stargazer lilies, the scent
of a sentence when it's ready

to speak. Relevant: the nuns folding
from *relevé* to *grand plié*
as they touch the stones

in Saint Gervais then kiss
the tips of their fingers
while worshippers lift
their arms, saguaro cacti
lost in the dark

or longhorn cattle swaying

                        in the nave. Here lies
cash, *lire*, a sachet of sighs: pay

                        to the account of *I'll*: yesterday,
here, *hier* and *ici*, the icy ache
                    of *ich*. You taught me
tart grammar, how to keep
                        thin slices of apple on edge

in *crème pâtissière* the way words
                        remain *en pointe* in a poem. Write
to me here: Dante@Kimosabe

Colors Are Not True

although all the labels say *deep colors*
bleed, the way cottonwoods sometimes turn
bright red when they are struck
by lightning. According to
the legend on the excavation map
beneath the church of St. Cecilia
in Rome, there are things
that are visible, things
not visible but about whose position
we are certain, and things thought
to have existed—like Mendelssohn's *Song*
Without Words, which we can hear
but not sing. Before the invention
of the five-line staff, neumes
flew above the text like crows, black
marks indicating the general shape but not
the exact notes to be sung, the way
the grocery list I found in London, jotted
on the back of a map, read:

Waitrose
1 kg oranges
I Yeo Valley butter
1/2 doz. eggs
1 loaf brown bread
1 jar raspberry jam
2 real rosy red apples & 4 pretend

Even when clouds gray the sky
on a winter day in Paris, there is
as Henry James said, *a presence*
in what is missing: nuance
keeps leading me back
to *nue* until all the *if's* of Eiffel
tower me.

Bon Voyage

> *People do not die for us immediately, but remain bathed in*
> *a sort of aura of life which bears no relation to true im-*
> *mortality but through which they continue to occupy our*
> *thoughts in the same way as when they were alive. It is as*
> *though they were traveling abroad.*
>
> Marcel Proust

My father never traveled
to France, but now lives
in Paris on the rue Mouffetard.
Each morning, early, he strolls
to Calixte and waits for croissants
to come out of the oven, then walks up
for breakfast to the tip of Ile Saint-Louis,
where he can gaze across the Seine at the back
of Notre Dame, while he reads *Le Monde*
without knowing any French. For lunch,
he orders a rare steak and a bottle
of Vacqueyras, followed by
a wedge of Roquefort, while he listens in
on conversations: the women seated by him
plan to spend the day shopping, searching
for pants that are more
forgiving. Later, as he walks
across the city, he snaps his fingers, singing
Hey diddle diddle, The cat and the fiddle,
The cow jumped over the moon, the way
he came up the stairs to wake me
when I was a child, keeping

in mind what Augustine said
of memory: *With my tongue silent*
and my throat making no sound, I can sing
what I wish. By evening he will have
arrived at Ryst-Dupeyron on the rue du Bac
to taste Armagnac—each bottle lined up
by year—from present to past. In spring, he plans
to go to London, thinks that perhaps
if the weather is good, my mother
might come.

History

Mallarmé said that Loie Fuller, with the wing
                of her skirt, created space
like the new convertible
                brought home by the neighbors
                on our block: at first a question mark
in the sky, then rising above them
                half a parenthesis until only
a comma was left behind, the shape
                of their hands as they waved
                down the street. "We ought to say a feeling
of *and*, a feeling of *if*, a feeling of
                but, and a feeling of *by*," William James
claimed, "quite as readily as we say
                a feeling of blue or a feeling
                of cold," but Leonardo's double-helix
staircase at Chateau Chambord wraps
                its arms around its own quiet
center, makes sure that the person going
                up and the one coming down
                never meet. The empty spaces, Conrad
said of maps, are the most
                interesting places because they are
what will change. So was it he
                who invented pinto horses, taught
                the mockingbird to keep not one
but two blank patches beneath
                its wings? We could hear

the car radio as they drove
         away, Elvis insisting *I'll be yours*
         through all the years, 'til the end
of time. From Latin *cor*,
                  for *heart*, to remember
in Spanish, *recordar*, means to pass
         once more through the heart
         the way the blood keeps coming
back for another tour, another
                  spin around the block. The yellow-
orange sash flapping past the window
         was memorable, a memorial, so much
         like an oriole or the scarf that keeps
circling the past's held
                  note: parked by the curb, the wisteria
was all ears, a hysteria of listening.

Nigh Clime

Who remembers the waving hinge, how
the spine of a book or elm could limn
the locale of *gee* and *hmm* and *oh*, tingle
with the *nom* of its genome chill as if Patsy Cline
were at the helm of the angelic galleon, singing
I'm crazy, crazy for feeling so blue.
                              When the long
is gone and the curtain opens
its glee like leaves in April, we'll mingle
like scenery and ogle o'er ego and e'en, the glim
of ago.
                    We still come helloing up the lingo
hill, its chenille lawn aching
with echo: omen, a lien
on our line. Lean your nog
against mine own and lift the hem
of home, not inchmeal but once: your chin
on its agile cello, your leg nigh
in the niche of time.

Pietà

It was the end
of an era, the end of
to be, Michelangelo's name
chiseled between her breasts

on the strip crossing her body
like the shoulder strap of a
seat belt, holding her
back from

the thrust of
grief. *I think he was
thinking that I thought* of
aspens shaking in full sunlight,

how noon is known when it casts
no shade. *What a difference
a day makes*, the old
song goes,

but what about
the difference an *l*
makes? You could have a
whole word or the entire world

except, of course, the sky above
Sangre de Cristo mountains
just after sunset when
the clouds line up

as if someone had
taken a black marker,
blocked out the parts we're
not supposed to read. In Hokusai's

painting, Li Po admires the flowing
wall of the world, a waterfall
so vertical that, turned
on its side, he sees

the horizon—
a blank sea in its lap
that cannot fold, envelop, or
wrap a body, lap over it the way the tide

urges its soft, rolling slaps. Gertrude Stein
said the sound of a paragraph
is emotional, her dog
lapping water

from a bowl:
like love, she says,
a paragraph is not pressed
for time. The highest form of divine

communication Dante calls *visibile*
parlare, visible speaking,
so Mary and Christ
continue in

conversation:
robed peak with a
flop of flesh in its lap, *V*
rising like the vowel of a coyote.

Brief Encounter

The story is *the only one*
　　　　　　I can tell and the only one I can

　　　　　　never tell, she says after she has left
her lover for the last time, in voiceover

to her husband, *the only one I can tell*
　　　　　　and the only one I can never

　　　　　　tell. "So help me with this,"
he says, "you're a poetry addict—

it's Keats: 'When I behold
　　　　　　upon the night's starred face

　　　　　　huge cloudy symbols of
a high _____' . . . seven letters,

beginning with *r*." *reading regalia*
　　　　　　rosette rotunda royalty rapture I didn't think

　　　　　　such violent things could happen
to ordinary people, she says, *radiant*

raccoon, raveled rivulet raiment
　　　　　　release although weeks ago she and her lover

sat in a dark theatre and watched the preview
of a film announced in flickering font

on the screen: *Flames of Passion—Coming*
                Shortly. The chords of Rachmaninoff draw

            dark lines across their faces, cancel
conversation like the diagonal trains

that slice the rectangular frames of film
                in two as they arrive and depart

            from Milford Junction station which, once
the lovers kiss, becomes a soundproof

room *reprise redwing refusal, recount rhubarb*
                reserve, reverse rustles refrain Hurrying

            home in the train she sees her face
facing her face in the window, racing

with darkened trees like the fragrant
                pages of a rampant book.

⚜

Afternoon

On the front porch, the mud cups of barn swallows
hold up the eaves, push-up bras the swallows keep
        slipping into like boomerangs sliding back
to a hand. My mother taught me how to make
        a fist, fingernails tucked inside, how to slip
my hand through nylon stockings
        without a snag. At the street light where
someone has thrown a stone and knocked out
        a corner of glass, the sparrow enters
her nest as we head into the theater
        for a matinee. I knew it was time
to take a break from writing poems
        when the woman at the bank asked what kind of
form I needed to have notarized, and I said *power*
        of eternity. So let's slip into something more
comfortable, like character or your native tongue,
        and then later, after dinner, we can slip out
early. But how far can the stargazer lilies walk
        in their orange velvet slippers? All the way
to *Point Zéro*, the point from which all distances
        are measured in France, if they are thinking of
Elizabeth Taylor in *Cat on a Hot Tin Roof*, leaning
        against the door frame in her tight white
slip. The old films often flickered
        and skipped, even occasionally slipped in
a blank screen. It's how the world would look
        through the eye of a lizard or bird: some nictitating
membrane swept across like a curtain
        at *The End* as we slip from consciousness into

oblivion—an act of not exactly forgiveness
        but an official forgetting that precedes
what's then forgotten.

Pallino, Pallone

On behalf of life, its befogged aioli
logic, its belief a-go-go, and the chief coifed
geological good, like Beatrice, *I come*
from where I most desire
to return. To have a small ball
in Italian, *avere il pallino di*, is to be crazy
about something: a filched lifeblood
bagel, a big illogical loggia, Childe Cedilla
or the first of July when the coho flailed
in the lief ago. But if it is
a big ball, *essere nel pallone* means
to lose it: Bah, Fidelio, send it back
to Chef Gigolo, tell him I am a beige foal
afield in a folio of age. Bring me
agile, biologic bail for my icefall hood
and a hedged, bifocal feel. An aloof
child, failed achoo, lilac-hoofed
loaf—with my big ideological
foliage, my haloed half, I am the alibi
of oblige, my hobby is ball.

Note

They wrote to say they'd found my mother *wondering*
in the garage—like entering the ethereal sphere,
I thought: *drawing near to its desire, so deeply*
is our intellect immersed that memory
cannot follow after it, as if desire were a fugitive
dye made from the blue stars of the forget-me-
not and hell could be defined as that which cannot be
forgotten, the damned condemned to go on
like Paolo and Francesca in desire but unable to
recognize what could move them so

      *   *   *

When I was a child, my mittens were attached
to each other, their cord running under
my coat from hand to hand like the blue
veins in the clear plastic Invisible
Man I assembled in the basement, and after
he left assisted living, my friend's father
kept asking, What if my mother dies
again? What, I thought, if she slips off
like a glove

      *   *   *

              In paradise,
Dante says, we will have only a memory
of having had a memory, now lost
like the photograph of my mother's great

grandfather printed from a negative made
from a photograph of a negative, which we
Xeroxed for keeps: it's the same old
story of the Perseids, their gray hair
streaking the sky the way ethereal
is streaked by real

*   *   *

Like denizens
of the cadenza, cicadas scratching
their cicatrices, a star shines until day
begins to lighten the sky, the shining
gone though the star remains, not
shining but not yet gone, still
moving across the heavens right up
to the moment the sky turns
sky blue.

One Speaks of Divine Things on a Sky-Blue Field

as the birds fly in to hear
St. Francis speak in Giotto's fresco, their bodies turning
transparent before they touch the ground
so the blue sky beyond them
can be seen: *sweet color*

of oriental sapphire that spread
above Dante as he climbed up out of Hell. Coming in
for a landing in late evening, five jets
line up along the horizon and
hang like golden wasps

above the azure
lights of the runway. Their contrails litter the spheres,
the *pentimenti* of a pleated skirt: impossible
to iron as the pleats of memory, pressed
together then splayed

like music
from an accordion. According to Leonardo, the earth
is moved by the weight of a tiny bird
resting upon it. At either end
of Giuliano's tomb

in the Medici Chapel,
Michelangelo placed *Day* and *Night,* as if the body were
some large leather suitcase, a portmanteau
opening into two hinged
compartments: *mezzo-*

giorno, mezzaluna, era
and its *errata.* In Giotto's frescoes, you sometimes see
the edges of *la giornata,* the space that can be
painted in a day, before
the plaster dries.

Le Plaisir

after Max Ophüls

The heart doesn't need suspenders, like the kites
flown by those who gathered at the end
of the Ile de la Cité to pull down
and back on invisible strings.

                      Before leaving
for the Third Crusade, Phillipe Auguste
wanted to protect Paris, so he built
a wall around it in the shape
of a heart, rising

like the wave of Bernini's *Apollo and Daphne*, forever
at its peak: transparent skin of stone, water
seen through to light, never
arriving at a shore

though coming—as the ones say who bend to watch
the drawing sketched in crosshatch
and shade by the woman seated
below—to life.

Once each year in early summer, in *le temps des
cerises*, even the hearts of pigeons
ripen, and *coeur de pigeon*
cherries hang, parachutes

on the verge of sky,

               but the heart doesn't need
suspenders, just as the people practicing
tai chi on the tip of the Ile
didn't need kites:

               they wanted the perfect balance
of walls, of the copper repoussé apostles
above them walking slowly down,
poised on the runway

beneath Notre Dame's spire. Soldiers entering Paris
never saw the shape of Phillipe Auguste's
desire, thought only that it would
not fall. At the end

               of *Le Plaisir*, silent lovers glide
along a beach, where the mortared sky
and sea push their gray stones
near: children tug kites,

               hold them like shields
against the sky while a voice nearby
decides *le Bonheur n'est pas
gai*. But if Voltaire

was right, and *l'écriture est la peinture de la
voix*, let the kites fly into red like
words, like the *coeur
de pigeon* cherries
               hanging amid green-veined
leaves, no stems attached.

Wont To Do

As it turns morning into light, you can hear
the earth creak on its axis, release the red *cheek*
cheek cheek of a cardinal.

———————————

Matisse's   *Luxe, Calme   et Volupté*:   clicks
on a keyboard, the ticking   of a clock, while   the naked bathers
go on like   melody beneath the sun's   cymbal, all that remains
of the fireworks rocket   stuck in the sand as if   it were a tree, its tip
splayed   like the barrel   of a shotgun too tightly   choked.
The center of   the painting   is silent: a small boat
with its sail   X   beached   on the red bank
of pleasure—its hyphenated   shore—the way   the memory of
pleasure   moors in the brain—violet,   yellow, orange, green bricks
mortared   with the white   of day. In the distance, the hills
hump like the heads   of crocodiles, slide   into the sea.

———————————

When she turned 87, my aunt spoke in sentences, long
and chiseled like the paths worn by the hooves
of cows on the hillside, switchbacks
winding up towards a peak as in Cézanne's
nonfinito paintings, where you can see

———————————

what isn't there. When night blooms,
it's serious: the poplar spills
soprano and warns the grackles
of my heart.

———————————

In medieval rhetoric, the path or way through
a text is called *ductus*, as in duct
and aqueduct: John of Patmos
must finally eat
the book.

———————————

Fill like April with chartreuse, swell
against the sky's gunmetal blue.

———————————

It's where we dwell, Dante says:
*cut off from hope, we go on
in desire*, always close
to won't.

Evening

Uncle Osie showed me how to lean
the chisel into the lathe, make the chair leg
curve as strips curled off the long rod
of walnut the way Dante's invented verb
dislagarsi makes the mountain of Purgatory rise up
out of the lake: it un-lakes itself while God keeps
turning his lathe with a Florentine form
of the verb *torniare* and makes the world above
inform the world below. *Wider*
than a mile, for sure, the Milky Way, and waiting
just around the bend, where my grandfather
said everything was, planted like hostages
who called the hostas *Moon River* for the blaze
their leaves rake across the dark
the way *possibility* laces Purgatory, plenary
or partial indulgences adding up like frequent
flier miles. In Purgatory, it's always late
summer, after supper, the cicadas ratcheting up
their cocktail shakers while the gloss
I've painted on the white picket fence runs off
in long drips and the pots of red geraniums you call
planets ascend the front porch steps. To the Good Humor man
just making his way down our street, we shout
Wait! And to the scuffed gloves that once leafed through
trees, turning beneath the maple, *Everyone*
in favor, hold up your hand.

Dark Spots

In the late nineteenth century, some photographers

claimed not only to capture images
of loved ones from beyond

the grave but to be able to photograph memories

of the deceased, their auras still glowing
around the bereaved,

as if to capture light reflected off a body could preserve

that body over time, as Beatrice explains
the presence of the dark

spots on the moon to Dante in *Paradiso*: how

the brightness of a celestial body
reveals the angelic

gladness that quickens the body, *letizia* that shines as joy

shines through an eye. *Visit Fort
Courage—Take Pictures*

of the Past, the billboards across Arizona advised,

and at the base of the mountain in
New Mexico, a note taped

to the gasoline pump read, *Hold tight to your money—the wind*

will carry it away. In the snapshot of
my grandmother in her

casket, wearing the Elizabethan collar and permed

curls she never wore, my mother
gazes through her

to a planet she always knew existed but which, without

the darkness, she could never see
before. They call

some bruises *shiners* like the violet stars of the Rose of Sharon

that come out in the morning and shine
all day in their leaf-black

shade, shade carved into the yard like fish scales covering

the sarcophagus in Sant'Apollinare in
Classe near Ravenna

or the stiff, veined hands of the sycamore stretched wide

in applause, the Italian gesture
of mourning.

View From My Father's Grave

The Confederate soldier must stand
for something, rifle pointed all these years
at the sky, while the Virginia creeper
and poison ivy sneak off
to the woods, where owls
answer every question
with a question.

                   Geese lift off, beginning
their long migration, as they do
each morning; in the sky, they form
the shape of the patch on my father's
sleeve. He's on leave, home
in 1944 and pressed
against my mother after
their wedding, their hands clasped
as if ready to dance.

                   What if they fall
out of the sky? There will be one
fewer letter in the alphabet. Loops
of exhaust plume the blue
with their *Will you*
marry me? like the swath
of razor down his Barbasol cheek.

                   How far down
do all the stones bear his name? We can
translate the weather's hocus-pocus
from its ancient Latin text—*cirrus*
cumulus nimbus cumulonimbus
nimbostratus—but not the scar

of light in Giorgione's *Tempest*, scribbled
on the sky where some god's been
testing his pen to see if it will
write. It's the Fourth of July: rockets
and starbursts scratch the night. Hold
a match to the black tablet
of each Magic Snake and let it etch
its long *S* across the sidewalk's blank, grow
hair like the dead or the limbs
of live oak. Let fireflies swerve, erase
the dark with their bright
fists of brief.

Item:

a beautiful hours, very well
and richly illuminated. The yarzeit candle

beats its yellow heart
all night, and the next morning

the ginkgo loses all of its leaves
at once. In 185 AD,

Chinese astronomers witnessed
what they called a *guest star*

that appeared in the sky and lingered
for eight months, the first documented

observation of a supernova, death
of a distant star. After his mother

died, my father arrived at her house
to find only a thimble

on the windowsill, erect
as a nipple. And when he

died, I found hanging, dry stone
in his shed, a shrink-wrapped

T-bone steak. *Item:* I saw
the swallowtail butterfly pull nectar

down its throat from the bush
called *butterfly*, watched its pages flutter

on that windless day until a passing
robin snapped them shut. As if opening

a book, they'll pull back the sheet
from my chest to find, where a pair of

pink doves once blinked, two
eyebrows, raised.

How to Know When the Dead Are Dead

Some crimes of early modern Europe were specific
to the night: keeping a public house open
too late, disturbing the peace, lantern smashing, dueling

at dusk or dawn, grave robbing, and walking
without a light. So fireflies, rising like embers
from the earth, members of the family

Lampyridae, Greek for "shining ones," still blink
their way through the night. Although they obey
God's first command, when the lights go out

do they stay?
    Upon election, the Pope takes
a new name, his old Christian name never

heard in the Vatican again until he lies
dead: the chamberlain then comes to his side
and calls him three times by the name

he once bore.
    To be sure the dead are dead,
Greeks would cut off a finger, Slavs rubbed bodies

with warm water for an hour, while Hebrews wait
for putrefaction because even without hands, the dove
still plays her flute. There are other ways,

of course, to know: the dead don't place bets, leave
their dinner untouched. Then just before the sky goes
dark, bats fly out like a pail of water tossed

from the eaves.
                        Even and thin but yellow with age, there can be
pleadings, an appeal or trial, a letter, dispatch, or note,

something summarized or abbreviated: *brief*
which in Scotland is called
a memorial.

Errand

My father and I have gone out because we are out
　　　　　　　of milk and *on every street corner you hear*
silver bells playing on the Pontiac's radio *wherever*
　　　　　two or three are gathered in my name, which I'm writing
　　　　　with my finger in the fog that has condensed
on the inside of the windshield while we wait
　　　　　　　for the light to turn green. And the empty
metal baskets *do* ring as we enter
　　　　　the bright store, High's Dairy, where row
　　　　　after row of cold glass bottles line up their
shoulders like swimmers or wrestlers
　　　　　　　in the team photo. Back in the car, first my breath
was visible, then not, like the visions
　　　　　of saints or the hills up ahead as the fog lifts
　　　　　then thickens while I drive on Route 95, half
a century later. A statue of St. Anthony of Padua,
　　　　　　　patron saint of all things lost,
stands in Santa Maria in Trastevere. He holds
　　　　　the Christ child in his arms, scraps of paper
　　　　　with messages and notes covering his feet, tucked
in each crease of his robe and stuck on the spikes
　　　　　　　of the child's halo as if it were a satellite
　　　　　waiting to be launched into space.

Sweet Gum

sputniks hail the autumn lawn
                    while stars litter the sky
          without a word, although birds still steer

by the pinups of the gods,
                    constellations wearing nothing
         but seams. The ideogram

sun seen in the trees
                    becomes *east*, and we keep asterisks
         in the margin of the page,

buttons on a coat we might open
                    or close, as if my mother was wrong
         when she said *memories*

are kind of hard
                    to forget. In winter they turn
         white like dandelions, da Vinci's perfect

human body cartwheeling
                    down the page with just one breath,
         which is why Dali had to invent

the *Aphrodisiac Jacket*, black
                    smoking jacket studded with shot glasses
         filled with crème de menthe

so that passersby could
             take a drink: it's the kind of coat
      the damned might wear

at the bottom of Hell,
             where it's always
      winter and the eye sockets of upturned

faces become small cups
             in which their tears
      freeze. Leonardo finally believed

that because the eye does not
             truly know the edge
      of any body, terror and desire are likely

to be seen in the black chalk
             of *sfumato*—like the sway of a sauce
      when it's finished

with butter, or you in your scarves'
             dark varnish. It's what kept
      the damned from heaven:

of all the sins, the hardest
             to give up was the memory
      of sin.

Hail to Thee,

I write, my wrist nodding
               as it does when chopping leeks
         and garlic with a knife, then stirring
the soup, whose project—with farro,
               ceci, and nettles—is *to present life*
         as it has been forgotten. Sit a while
and wrest the awe from these rites; an era
               waits, wistful on the wire, while
         the priest holds up the host
as if it were the sun
               or moon, says *this is*
         my body, then blesses
and breaks it. When the sky
               is on a lark, *we look before*
         and after, lest we be struck
by *unpremeditated art:* Outside,
               the wet irises wait, waist-high
         in Shelley's *pale purple even*
while my father, in summer after
               supper, lifts each burning briquette
         with his tongs and holds it
deep in water until the black
               stops hissing and bubbles cease
         to rise. He places them on a sheet
of newsprint to dry, lined up
               the way the bodies of the dead
         wait for the Resurrection. *Bird,*

although *thou never wert*, arise: please

    rate your purchase, just as St. Augustine

  distinguished the eternal from

the human: our sentences

    have a beginning

  and an end—except for the one

he proposed for his own

    epitaph, once used by an ancient

  Roman whose tomb stood

next to the road: *When you read these words,*

    I speak, and your voice

  is mine.

Che Fai di Bello

They are burning the fields in
      Assisi, unearthing *tartufi* from beneath Umbrian oaks
for the umpteenth time. So slow

      they don't even shuffle, black
and swelling, *tartufi* think
      only of roots, just as the Islamic call

to prayer, *adhān*, is at the root
      of the word *permit*, as in *let someone
hear these words*, for which

      they will also need *udun*, the word
for *ear*. All summer
      the hornworm curves forward

like summer—San Marzano, Brandywine, Sweet
      Million, *Jaune Flammée*—consuming its own
path while the white larvae of the wasp

      cling to its back like saddlebags or unweaned
possums. The lily of
      the valley, too, lifts white stones overhead,

climbing its green ladder
      like Jacob's Ladder at the gym, which we continue to
climb though never any higher, the way

St. Catherine's head lifts forever
a half-step on the white marble slab
          where she lies in Santa Maria sopra

Minerva, curls of stone enclosing
          pink commas that held what she no longer
hears. And because she cannot speak

          in Giovanni di Paolo's painting, she holds out
her heart to Christ in order
          to exchange it for his, a handful of red

in tempera and gold on wood:
          *Che fai di bello oggi, What are you doing
today,* Italians ask when they meet

          on the streets of Rome, *What do you make
of the beautiful?* Although
          they're dead, the damned can see the open

notes of the white-throated
          sparrow notching the air like a pulse: *the way
his throat moves,* they say

          of Dante, *this one must be alive.* It lay in the rain
this morning, across new
          asphalt, a duller spot, cluster of dust the size

of a mouse I might not
          have seen except for the pink ear, the sound
it brought to mind.

Shade

As the air full of rain takes on rainbow
hues not of its own making but reflecting
the brightness of another, so the soul
of a shade, Statius explains to Dante
in Purgatory, is made visible like flame
following the shift and flicker of
its fire: the soul imprints itself
on the surrounding air to make it
resemble, reassemble the memory
of its body, just as the six hundred foot high
sandstone walls marbled in shades of
pink, of rose and red, and sometimes
veined in cobalt blue remember
the chasm of the Siq, the city of Petra
carved in its side. Copper—from Latin *cuprum*,
"from Cyprus"—in ancient times was mined
on the island of Cyprus, and the Greek
kutuhlpa meant "head with wings," so the unclaimed
cremated remains of those known as
the incurably insane at Oregon State Hospital
were sealed in copper canisters and placed
in an underground vault, forgotten and flooded
for fifteen years. Mold or lichen, phosphorescent
frost? A host of ashes coats the copper: cuprite,
azurite, malachite turn to verdigris, turquoise, atoll
green and the lapis lazuli seas of Hokusai seen
from outer space, the white seam of a shoreline
at every tropical copper beach, where the long news
of the body finally breaks. Like a necklace

at the edge of saline or alkaline lakes, crust

        of flour on the fingers or powder after surgical gloves

peel off, the pollen of catalpa blossoms remained

        on the tips long after our fingers slid

past the purple spots and yellow flares

        into each white frilly, unfurled urn:

we plucked them from the green-hearted

        leaves, chanting *witches' fingers, heads*

with wings, our hands held up like the claws

        of Hokusai's Great Wave, like St. Francis

receiving the stigmata or the hands

        my grandmother raised when she looked up

after she had finished kneading dough.

Ars Poetica

The shell of the papershell pecan can easily be broken
in one hand but is so thin it cannot be
written on, like the carapace
of the cicada, enclosing those hollow
abdomens that buckle their ribs
all night. We find them each morning:
notes hung by the nape
on hedges, the shape of their sound
lifted to a branch like the ex-voto
boti, their own life-size
wax effigies, which Florentines
in the Renaissance suspended—
as an offering or in thanks—from the vault
of Santissima Annunziata.
$\qquad\qquad\qquad$ Leonardo sought
to reconcile the apparent contradiction
between a static, lifeless
artifact and the enlivenment
it provokes, to understand how the words of
the dead go on speaking. No one ever knew
a pecan tree to die of old age, but because
even ink drying on paper takes part
in the process of aging, he thought the life
of a work of art must be
measured by its *vivacità*, how well
it can vivify a beholder—like Charles Ray's statue
of *Boy with Frog*, standing on the Grand Canal
in Venice, which must be protected
from assault, both day and night,

by a living person.

                         I once dreamed a word entirely
Baroque: a serpentine line of letters leaning
with the flourish of each touching the shoulder
of another so that one breath at the word's
beginning made them all collapse. *E spesso moiano
parlando*, Leonardo wrote: *we die, very often,
while we speak*, the way Common Swifts,
named from the Greek *without feet*, never settle
voluntarily on the ground but spend
their life, in faithful pairs from year
to year, in flight. They drink, eat, rest
and often mate on the wing: late
in the season they gather, circling in the air
above their nests, calling out
to each other as they ascend
to sleep.

Shadow of the Evening

Among the great things which are found among us,
the existence of Nothing is the greatest.

Leonardo da Vinci

Gondoliers in Venice push into the late
afternoon shade for *un'ombra*, something
cool to drink as shadows lean—elongated, bronze
like the 22" tall by 4" wide statue of a boy
wearing no clothes, no jewelry, nothing
to indicate rank, status, age, ploughed up
by a farmer in 1879 and used to poke the fire
until someone could finally see it was a 3rd century BC
Etruscan votive once placed with intention
like the indentation in tall grass where the deer
fell asleep last night.
                    Gabriele d'Annunzio called it
l'ombra della sera because the bronze
reminded him of the shadow
thrown by a human figure in the dying
light of the evening sun, as on that evening
in 1949 when my brother—he must have been
three—crawled over the front seat
of the car towards the back, reached for
the push-down handle of the door and
fell out, rolling down the road as my parents
sped by. My mother turned to grasp him
the way Dante keeps trying
to clasp a shade, wrapping her arms
around her own chest.

Revision

When the pasta is badly broken, we eat
maltagliati, and once we think
the risotto is done, we must still
make it creamy, *mantecare*. Because it was
never finished, Proust kept writing
in the margins of his drafts, and when
they were full, pasted small pieces of paper,
paperoles unfurling from the page as if

it had wings, could be released on parole
with a promise of words. *The past*, he claimed,
is hidden in some material object of which
we have no inkling, just as scientists maintain
that because a memory is altered each time
it's recalled, the original memory is the one

we can't know. In Michelangelo's crosshatching

and chiseling, the two-dimensional slowly
becomes three by the same math used
in the sentence *The royal We lives*
in Synecdoche, New York. But since when
is a sentence ever innocent? Phoebes
still wag from the wires like words we meant

to say, and Michelangelo's Prisoners
remain locked in stone because
we can't remember that they were
ever free. But if we have to misremember

in order to recall, what must we do
to forget? At the end of June, cabbage leaves begin
curving in toward one another. Soon they will
bury their head in their many hands.

Dessert

It's what will be
   set out once the table
has been cleared, from the French
     verb *desservir*, to unserve or remove
   what has been served. But should we use
service à la russe, in which one dish
   follows another, or *service à la*
française, everything served
     at once? Michelangelo's steps
   to the Laurentian Library have it
both ways: they come out
   to meet you like an open
package of Necco wafers, gray
     licorice scent rising, or a flipbook
   of the lower lip descending. While
they were reading, medieval monks
   murmured, lips vibrating as if each word
were a blossom and the world
     around them the amber memory
   of bees. How often our own lips
have passed each other
   on the street, although Bernini claims
a person's face looks most
     like that person the moment before
   and after he speaks. They rustle
like elves in the leaves, so the French
   call them *lèvres*, the levers, lapels

of the mouth, where we lapse

                    into ourselves. In the Capuchin catacombs

       of Palermo, the bodies of parishioners

dating far back in time

         are laid in rows hung on the walls

so that ascending from the depths

                 of the catacombs, one sees the clothing

       covering the bodies

regain its texture and color, the faces

       their individual features

as if each body were entering Chaucer's

              House of Fame, where all the voices

     of human beings rise from the earth

and assume the shape of those

       who spoke them. Like waves spreading

up the beach, their words keep

            getting thinner until it seems we might

      see though them, just before

they sink into sand. In Leonardo's *Mona Lisa*,

     for instance: is that a smile

or a simile? Since lips

          can be parted, Antony tells

     the messenger, *Speak to me*

home. On long car trips,

     I kept asking my parents, *Are we*

there yet? And they always

        replied, *almost, nearly,*

    close.

Almost Autumn

and the sky this morning already a December
sky in Venice, itself a closet lit only by a seam
of remembered light. The geese send their silhouettes

across it, evidence that something moves
on the other side. For weeks in May, pecan blossoms
streaked the air and we found out

what it was like to spend an entire season
in the Perseids, how God must have felt
creating the stars in an initial O, illuminated

in a fifteenth-century manuscript in Siena. So many
stars to touch on the iPad of the night, to name
as each turned into light: *wear, were,*

never, ere. Down here, I've been considering
whether these split-shingle cardinals are *mottled*
or *molting*—probably more like melting

in this late August heat. Not one pecan
survived the summer, though it's better perhaps not
to have them knocking on the roof all hours

of the night. I'm trying to see what some call
the bright side, how the sun does not
disappear: it's just the world turning

away. In the Sienese illumination, Earth's a gnarled
green marble, the center of zero, something shot
clear through to *seen*, but who inflated

the cosmos around it, tossed it out
like a blue plastic float? I still think God may be
holding up the hem of his gown as he reaches

for *Livia, livid, ever, seem*, until a slip
of his tongue lights up *oblivion, believe*. The mourning
dove has mounted to the peak

of the roof; impossible to say which side
she is rooting for. When the sky gets dark enough
for all the stars to be seen, what we'll need

is not some pleated ocean waving
adieu, but a word, the last
in French films: *Fin*, what we will use

to swim away.

Recall

She squeezed the trout until the mouth opened
                    like a plastic coin purse and held its hollow
in her hand, the mouth of a bottle she might

                    drink from, said *say ah, say a e i o u,* as she reached
her fingers down its throat, black patch, galactic
                    path where the hook curved like the left hook of

a comet or a hangnail of plaque snagged at the branch
                    of an artery, bent rod of the nibble or strike.
In *Purgatory*, God trolls his lures

                    through the heavens, *richiamo:* Recall the way
a lifeguard twirls his whistle, how stars spin
                    through space, flipping and flashing

as if they were *ricciarelli,*
                    cookies shaped like the almond eyes
of madonnas that keep calling me back

                    to Siena. *As a bird to its lure, as the bird*
at its call. Bachelard recalls how
                    the French baritone said it is impossible

to think the vowel sound *ah* without
                    tensing, tightening the vocal chords: *we read* ah
and the voice is ready to sing.

Notes

Dedication: Dante Alighieri, *Paradiso*, XXVIII, 3.

"*I Want to Talk About You*": after John Coltrane; Martin Williams, Review of *Africa/Brass* (Impulse! 1961) in *Down Beat*; Dante Alighieri, *The Inferno*.

"Colors Are Not True": with thanks to Adam and Nadia.

"Bon Voyage": Marcel Proust, *In Search of Lost Time: The Fugitive*; Saint Augustine, *Confessions*.

"History": William James, *The Principles of Psychology*; Elvis Presley, "Love Me Tender."

"*Pietà*": "I think he was thinking that I thought," from Dante Alighieri, *The Inferno*; "*visibile parlare,*" from Dante Alighieri, *Purgatorio*; Gertrude Stein, "Poetry and Grammar."

"*Brief Encounter*": after David Lean's film.

"*Pallino, Pallone*": "I come from where I most desire to return," from Dante Alighieri, *The Inferno*.

"Note": "drawing near to its desire…memory cannot follow after it," from Dante Alighieri, *Paradiso*.

"*One Speaks of Divine Things on a Sky-Blue Field*": Michelangelo's annotation to the autograph text of his poem "*Se dal cor lieto,*" in Leonard Barkan, *Michelangelo: A Life on Paper*; Leonardo da Vinci, *Notebooks*.

"*Le Plaisir*": Voltaire, "Orthography" in *Philosophical Dictionary*.

"*Item:*": *Belles Heures of Jean de France, Duc de Berry*.

"How to Know When the Dead Are Dead": Craig Koslofsky, *Evening's Empire: A History of the Night in Early Modern Europe*; "Even and thin but yellow with age," *Archaeologia: or, Miscellaneous tracts relating to antiquity*, 1796.

"*Hail to Thee,*": Percy Bysshe Shelley, "To a Skylark"; "to present life as it has been forgotten," Walter Benjamin, *Passagen-Werk*, in Susan Buck-Morss, *The Dialectics of Seeing: Walter Benjamin and the Arcades Project*; Saint Augustine, *Confessions*.

"Shade": David Maisel, *Library of Dust.*

"Ars Poetica": "*E spesso moiano parlando,*" Leonardo da Vinci, in Kenneth D. Keele and Carlo Pedretti, *Leonardo da Vinci: Corpus of the Anatomical Studies in the Collection of Her Majesty the Queen at Windsor Castle.*

"Shadow of the Evening": epigraph from Leonardo da Vinci, *Notebooks.*

"Dessert": Philippe-Alain Michaud, *Aby Warburg and the Image in Motion.*

"Almost Autumn": *God Creating the Stars in an Initial O*, Siena, 15th Century, Wildenstein Collection, Musée Marmottan, Paris.

"Recall": Dante Alighieri, *Purgatorio*; Gaston Bachelard, *The Poetics of Space.*

Acknowledgments

The American Scholar: "Nigh Clime," "Afternoon," "How to Know When the Dead Are Dead," "Recall"

The Cincinnati Review: "Sweet Gum"

Connotation Press, An Online Artifact: A Poetry Congeries: "Revision," "Colors Are Not True," "Errand," "Wont to Do"

FIELD: "*Pallino, Pallone*," "Evening," "Dessert"

Gulf Coast: "*Pietà*"

The Manhattan Review: "*One Speaks of Divine Things on a Sky-Blue Field*," "View From My Father's Grave," "Shadow of the Evening"

Michigan Quarterly Review: "*Le Plaisir*," "*Item:*"

New Ohio Review: "*I Want to Talk About You*"

Plume: "*Che Fai di Bello*," "*Hail to Thee*," "Ars Poetica"

Poetry London: "Shade," "Note," "*Brief Encounter*"

Slate: "Almost Autumn," "History"

Southwest Review: "Dark Spots"

Sycamore Review: "Per Your Request,"

"I Want to Talk About You" also appeared on *Best American Poetry* online, and "Dark Spots" and "*Item:*" on *Poetry Daily*. "*Che Fai di Bello*" was published in *The Plume Anthology of Poetry 2012*, and "Cache" in *The Plume Anthology of Poetry 2013*.

"*Le Plaisir*" and "*Item:*" received the 2012 Laurence Goldstein Poetry Prize.

My gratitude to the Guggenheim Foundation for their generous support of my work and to the National Endowment for the Humanities for supporting my studies in Florence at the NEH Summer Institute "Leonardo da Vinci: Between Science and Art." *Mille grazie* to our seminar director, Professor Francesca Fiorani. I am deeply grateful to the Lannan Foundation for offering me a Marfa Writers Residency, during which many of these poems were written.

About the Author

Angie Estes is the author of four previous books, most recently *Tryst* (2009), which was selected as one of two finalists for the 2010 Pulitzer Prize. Her second book, *Voice-Over* (2002), won the 2001 *FIELD* Poetry Prize and was also awarded the 2001 Alice Fay di Castagnola Prize from the Poetry Society of America. Her first book, *The Uses of Passion* (1995), was the winner of the Peregrine Smith Poetry Prize. The recipient of many awards, including a Guggenheim Fellowship, the Cecil Hemley Memorial Award from the Poetry Society of America, and a Pushcart Prize, she has received fellowships from the National Endowment for the Humanities, the National Endowment for the Arts, the Woodrow Wilson Foundation, the California Arts Council, and the Ohio Arts Council, and has been awarded artist residencies by The MacDowell Colony and the Lannan Foundation.